CW00672743

Published July 2007

ISBN 978 1 906008 10 9

© Middleton Press, 2007

Design Deborah Esher
Typesetting Barbara Mitchell

Published by
            Middleton Press
            Easebourne Lane
            Midhurst
            West Sussex
            GU29 9AZ
Tel: 01730 813169
Fax: 01730 812601
Email: info@middletonpress.co.uk
www.middletonpress.co.uk

Printed & bound by Biddles Ltd, Kings Lynn

KIDDERMINSTER TO SHREWSBURY

Vic Mitchell and Keith Smith

MP Middleton Press

HISTORICAL BACKGROUND

Shrewsbury had the Shrewsbury & Chester Railway from 1848 and the Shrewsbury & Birmingham Railway from 1849, while Kidderminster was served by the Oxford, Worcester & Wolverhampton Railway from 1852. The latter became part of the West Midland Railway in 1860 and the Great Western Railway in 1863. Shrewsbury was subject to several joint ventures and a notable independent operation, mentioned later under the heading South of Shrewsbury.

An Act for the Severn Valley Railway between Hartlebury and Shrewsbury was passed in 1853 and the route opened on 1st February 1862. Trains were provided by the WMR; the GWR eventually took control of the company in 1872. Coalport had received a service a little earlier, when the London & North Western Railway opened its branch from the north in 1861.

The GWR opened a link between Kidderminster and Bewdley on 1st June 1878. There were no major changes until nationalisation in 1948, when the GWR became the Western Region of British Railways. The lines in the area were transferred to the London Midland Region on 1st January 1963.

Passenger service between Bewdley and Shrewsbury was withdrawn on 9th September 1963 and the 1864 Tenbury-Bewdley line through Cleobury Mortimer was closed in 1965. The 1862-64 lines to Buildwas also lost their passenger services in 1963.

A Hartlebury-Bewdley-Kidderminster service was provided between 1963 and 5th January 1970. The line between Hartlebury and Stourport Power Station remained open for freight until 1980 and the spur between Kidderminster and the sugar factory at Foley Park lasted until 1984.

The Severn Valley Railway Society was formed on 6th July 1965 to reopen the line between Hampton Loade and Bridgnorth. This was achieved on 23rd May 1970, coal traffic south of Alveley having ceased in 1969. The SVR became a company in 1967 and pursued the purchase of the route south to Foley Park.

The train service was extended from Hampton Loade to Highley on 12th April 1974 and on to Bewdley on 18th May of that year. Extension to Kidderminster took place on 30th July 1984.

PASSENGER SERVICES

The first timetable offered four trains, weekdays only, between Hartlebury and Shrewsbury. From 1878, there was also one on Sundays and five trains were also provided between Kidderminster and Bewdley. This number was reduced to four by 1880, but, by 1902, both routes were enjoying five weekday services, plus three extras north to Bridgnorth. A few originated at Worcester.

A similar pattern continued until World War II, although the Sunday train was limited mainly to the 1930s. Four or five weekday trains were provided at most stations until closure, plus a few short workings. The number of trains starting at Kidderminster instead of Hartlebury increased over the years. In the final period, a triangular route was operated between these places via Bewdley on weekdays only, the June 1968 timetable showing two such through trains, plus six short workings, mostly in the peak hours. A Kidderminster-Bewdley-Stourport service had been provided by railmotors from 1905, but this had declined to one trip by World War II.

Two trains were provided on Summer Sundays between Birmingham and Bridgnorth from the 1950s until closure; they were used mainly by fishermen. In the 1964 timetable, there were also six trains on Sundays between Birmingham and Stourport-on-Severn via Bewdley.

The revived SVR initially operated at weekends only, but the services gradually expanded and the timetables have been steadily developed to meet seasonal demands.

July 1878

SEVERN VALLEY.—Great Western.

Up.	Week Days.								Sn
Fm. Wrexhm, 20	mrn	mrn	mrn	mrn	aft	aft	aft	aft	mrn
CHESTER 20 d	gov	....	....	9 10	....	2 0	....	4 25	9 40
Shrewsbury dp	6 40	....	....	1110	....	3 30	....	7 0	5 5
Berrington	6 50	....	....	1120	....	3 40	....	7 10	5 15
Cressage..	7 0	....	....	1128	....	3 49	....	7 20	5 25
Much Wenlock d	....	....	....	9 52	....	3 20	....	7 10	....
Much Wenlock a	1015	....	....	1152	....	4 55	....	7 47	aft
Buildwas ..[ley	7 10	....	....	1140	....	4 0	....	7 30	5 35
Ironbdg & Bros-	7 16	....	....	1145	....	4 8	....	7 35	5 40
Coalport 154..	7 21	....	....	1150	....	4 13	....	7 40	5 45
Linley	7 28	....	....	1158	....	4 20	....	a	5 52
Bridgnorth....	7 40	9 0	....	1210	....	4 35	....	8 0	6 4
Eardington	7 46	....	....	a	....	a	....	a	6 10
Hampton Lode	7 51	....	....	1223	....	4 48	....	8 13	6 16
Highley	7 58	....	....	1230	....	4 55	....	8 20	6 23
Arley	8 5	....	....	1238	....	5 2	....	8 26	6 30
Tenbury and Bewdley Branch Woofrtn d	7 10	....	1015	1150	2 57	....	4 35	....	....
Easton C. .	7 17	....	1022	1158	3 4	....	4 43	....	....
Tenbury ,,	7 26	....	1031	12 5	3 12	....	4 50	....	....
Newnhm B	7 35	....	1040	1214		....	4 57	....	....
Neen Sollrs	7 42	....	1047	1221	3 25	....	5 6	....	....
Cleobury M	7 53	....	1059	1232	3 36	....	5 17	....	....
Wyre Forst	7 59	....	....	1239	....	....	5 24	....	....
Bewdley ..	8 15	....	1114	1250	3 51	....	5 35	....	....
Kidrmnstr	8 25	....	1128	1 5	4 2	....	5 47	....	....
Bewdley	8 15	9 2	....	1256	....	5 13	5 37	8 34	6 40
Stourport......	8 23	9 23	....	1 5	....	5 23	5 51	8 43	6 50
Hartlebry J. 24	8c30	9 34	....	1 14	....	5 31	6 4	8 50	7c0
Droitwich 212	9c0	9 46	....	1 59	....	5 51	6 20	9 19	7c18
Fearnall Heath .	9c8	....	....	....	....	....	....	9 29	7c27
Worcester 25..	9c15	9 55		1 51	5 25	6 2	6 30	9 35	7c33
OXFORD 25 a	1150	1150	...	4 25	....	8 50	8 56	....	....
21 LNDN (Pad.),,	1 50	1 50	....	4 15	....	1048	1048	....	....

Down.	Week Days.						Sn
Paddingtn Sta.	mrn	gov	mrn	mrn	aft	aft	gov
LONDON 18 dep	....	....	5 50	10 0	....	2 15	mrn
OXFORD 24 ,,	....	....	8 15	1150	....	4 10	....
Worcester ..dep	7 50	8c55	1045	2 5	3 40	6 10	9c2
Fearnall Heath..	7 57	9c1	....	....	....	....	9c9
Droitwich	8 4	9c9	1055	2 17	....	6 22	9c17
Hartlebury Jun	8 15	9c38	11 7	2 40	....	6 50	9c40
Stourport	8 22	9 46	1114	2 48	....	6 58	9 48
Bewdley	8 30	9 56	1121	3 0	....	7 10	9 56
Tenbury and Bewdley Branch Kidermnstr	....	10 3	1 20	2 45	5 25	6 50	....
Bewdley dp	....	1015	1 32	3 12	5 36	7 18	....
Wyre Forst	....	1027	1 44	3 24	....	7 30	....
Cleobury M.	....	1035	1 52	3 35	5 53	7 38	....
Neen Sollars	1,2,3 class.	1048	2 2	3 44	6 2	7 47	....
Newnham B		1054	2 8	3 50	....	7 53	....
Tenbury arr		11 2	2 16	3 58	6 14	8 1	....
Easton C. ..		1113	2 27	4 8	6 22	8 11	....
Woofferton		1120	2 35	4 15	6 29	8 17	....
Arley	8 38	10 5	1129	3 9	....	7 19	10 5
Highley	a	1013	....	a	....	7 26	1012
Hampton Lode..	8 47	1022	1140	3 21	....	7 34	1019
Eardington......	8 52	1031	....	a	....	a	1027
Bridgnorth	9 0	104b	1150	3 38	....	7 55	1034
Linley	9 9	11 6	....	a	....	a	1046
Coalprt 154[ley	9 15	1116	....	3 53	....	8 11	1053
Ironbdg & Brose-	9 21	1122	....	4 4	....	8 17	1059
Much Wenlock d	8 0	9 52	....	3 20	....	7 10	....
Much Wenlock a	1015	1152	....	4 55	....	9 29	....
Buildwas	9 28	1135	....	4 10	....	8 25	11 4
Cressage	9 36	1145	....	4 20	....	8 35	1114
Berrington [154	9 46	1155	....	a	....	8 45	1124
Shrewsbury 19	9 57	12 5	....	4 40	....	8 55	1135
CHESTER 18 ar	1130	2 2	....	7 10	....	1243	5 45

a Stop when required. b Departs at 10 50 mrn. c 1,2,3 class between those Stations.

December 1902

WORCESTER, BEWDLEY, TENBURY, BRIDGNORTH, MUCH WENLOCK, & SHREWSBURY.—G.W.

Miles frm Worcester	Down.	Week Days.															Sn
	Paddington Station,	mrn	mrn	mrn	mrn	mrn	mrn	mrn	mrn	aft	aft	aft	aft	aft	aft	aft	mrn
	LONDON 38 ....dep.	....	....	....	....	....	5 40	9 50	....	1 45	....	1 45	....	1 50	4 45	....	....
	OXFORD 56 .... "	....	....	....	....	....	7 58	1120	1155	3 8	....	3 8	....	3 42	6 3	....	....
	Worcester (Shrub Hill) dep.	....	7 20	....	9 45	9 55	1040	1257	2 28	4 45	....	5c10	....	6 20	7 44	....	9 10
2½	Fernhill Heath	....	7 28	....	9 51	....	....	1 4	2 37	4 51	....	....	....	....	6p41	....	9 17
5¾	Droitwich	....	7 34	....	9 57	10 6	1048	1 10	2 43	4 57	....	....	....	6 30	7 52	....	9 23
11¼	Hartlebury	....	7 51	....	1011	....	11 5	1 45	3 10	5 23	....	....	6 0	7 2	7o40	9 30	9 45
14½	Stourport........	....	8 1	....	1019	....	1113	1 51	3 16	5 35	....	....	6 9	7 13	....	9 36	9 53
17¼	Bewdley (below) ......arr.	....	8 7	....	1025	1113	1119	1 57	3 22	5 42	....	....	6 15	7 20	8 46	9 42	9 59
—	BIRMINGHAM * 52. dep.	....	....	7 10	9 2	1015	9a35	1235	1h19	....	....	4 25	Stop	5 58	7 10	....	8 5
—	52 " (New St.) "	....	....	....	8 48	....	9a25	1230	....	....	....	4 20		....	....	....	....
—	*Tenbury and Bewdley Branch.* Kidderminster ....dep.	7 50	....	8 40	1015	11 5	....	1 50	....	....	Saturdays only.	5 39	....	7 8	8 38	....	9 28
—	Bewdley .... arr.	7 58	....	8 50	1023	1113	....	1 58	....	....		5 47	....	7 16	8 46	....	9 59
—	(see below) dep.	....	....	8 53	1035	....	....	2 8	....	....		5 49	....	7 27	....	....	....
20¾	Wyre Forest	....	....	9 6	1048	....	....	2 19	....	....		6 0	....	7 38	....	....	....
23½	Cleobury Mortimer....	....	....	9 14	1056	....	....	2 26	....	....		6 8	....	7 46	....	....	....
27¼	Neen Sollars	....	....	9 24	11 4	....	....	2 33	....	....		6 17	....	7 54	....	....	....
29½	Newnham Bridge......	....	....	9 29	11 9	....	....	2 39	....	....		6 23	....	8 0	....	....	....
32¾	Tenbury ....arr.	....	....	9 35	1115	....	....	2 45	....	....		6 31	....	8 7	....	....	....
35	Easton Court † .... "	....	....	9 48	1125	....	....	3 51	....	....		6 45	....	8 16	....	....	....
37¾	Woofferton 388 to 391	....	....	9 55	1130	....	....	3 56	....	....		6 50	....	8 32	....	....	....
—	Bewdley ....dep.	....	8 15	....	1034	1115	1125	2 6	3 25	....		....	....	7 30	8 51	....	10 2
20½	Arley	....	8 23	....	1043	1123	1133	2 14	3 33	....		....	....	7 38	8 59	....	1011
23	Highley	....	8 30	....	1050	1130	1140	2 21	3 40	....		....	....	7 44	9 5	....	1017
25¼	Hampton Loade	....	8 36	....	1056	1137	1147	2 27	3 46	....		....	....	7 50	9 11	....	1023
27¾	Eardington	....	8 41	....	11 1	....	1155	2 32	3 52	....		....	....	7 56	d	....	1029
29¾	Bridgnorth........	....	8 52	....	1112	1145	12 1	2 41	4 1	....		....	....	8 8	9 21	....	1037
34	Linley	....	9 0	....	1121	....	....	2 49	4 10	....		....	....	8 16	....	....	1046
36¾	Coalport 397........	....	9 6	....	1128	....	....	2 55	4 17	....		....	....	8 23	....	....	1053
38¾	Iron Bridge and Broseley	....	9 13	....	1135	....	....	3 1	4 23	....	6 0	....	aft	8 28	....	....	1058
40	Buildwas 53........	....	9 21	....	1142	....	....	3 7	4 29	....	6 5	....	7 55	8 34	....	....	11 4
43¼	Much Wenlock.. arr.	....	1013	....	1215	....	....	3 53	4 54	....	6 30	....	....	9 54	....	....	....
—	dep.	....	8 53	....	....	....	....	2 50	....	....	4 30	....	7 35	....	....	....	....
44	Cressage	....	9 29	....	1150	....	....	3 15	4 37	....	6 13	....	8 3	8 42	....	....	1112
48	Berrington ....[388 to 391	....	9 41	....	12 1	....	....	3 27	4 47	....	6 21	....	8 14	8 52	....	....	1122
52½	Shrewsbury39,386,387,ar	....	9 50	....	1212	....	....	3 35	4 55	....	6 30	....	8 23	9 0	....	....	1130

June 1922

WORCESTER, BEWDLEY, BRIDGNORTH, BUILDWAS, and SHREWSBURY.—Great Western.

Miles.	Down.	Week Days only.										
		mrn	mrn	mrn	mrn	aft	aft	aft	aft	aft	aft	
	Worcester(Shrub H)dep.	....	Mondays only.	7 0	9 35	1250	2 10	3 50	4 47	5B12	7 17	....
2¼	Fernhill Heath	....		7 6	....	1256	2 16	....	4 53	....	6a26	....
5½	Droitwich	....		7 12	9 47	1 6	2 24	4 3	5 1	5c23	7 28	....
11¼	Hartlebury ...... arr.	....		7 25	9 59	1 19	2 36	4 16	5 14	....	7 40	....
	dep.	....		7 28	10n5	1 35	2n45	4 30	5 35	....	7n45	....
14¼	Stourport	....		7 38	10n12	1 42	2n53	4 40	5 42	....	7n52	....
16¾	Bewdley 90, 99....arr.	....		7 45	10n18	1 49	3n0	4 46	5 49	....	7n58	....
—	98 BIRMINGHM(S.H.)dep.	m	....	5 40	9 43	1 0	....	3 45	....	5 5	7 5	....
—	90 KIDDERMINSTR .. "	5 30	6 10	7 40	10 45	1 55	....	4 40	....	5 47	7 58	....
—	Bewdley ....dep.	5 41	6 23	7 53	10 58	2 8	....	5 0	6 2		8 12	....
20½	Arley	5 50	6 30	8 0	11 6	2 15	....	5 8	6 9		8 19	....
22¾	Highley	5 56	6 37	8 7	11 13	2 23	....	5 15	6 16		8 26	....
25	Hampton Loade........	....	6 42	8 12	11 19	2 29	....	5 21	6 21		8 31	....
27¼	Eardington........	....	....	8 17	11 24	2 34	....	5 27	6 26		....	....
29½	Bridgnorth ...... arr.	....	6 50	8 22	11 30	2 40	....	5 33	6 31		8 41	....
	dep.	....	....	8 25	11 35	2 45	....	5 40	6 35		m	....
33¾	Linley	....	....	8 33	11 43	2 53	....	5 48	6 43		....	....
36½	Coalport 446	....	....	8 39	11 50	2 59	....	5 54	6 49		....	....
38¾	Iron Bridge and Broseley	....	....	8 44	12 3	3 5	....	6 5	6 57		....	....
39¾	Buildwas 94	....	....	8R58	12 10	3 11	....	6 15	7 4		....	....
43¼	Cressage ....[454	....	....	9 4	12 17	3 18	....	6 24	7 12		....	....
47¾	Berrington...(450, 452,	....	....	9 14	12 24	3 25	....	6 33	7 21		....	....
52	Shrewsbury † 84 ..arr.	....	....	9 25	12 32	3 35	....	6 46	7 30		....	....

Miles.	Up.	Week Days only.												
		mrn	mrn	mrn	mrn	mrn	mrn	aft	aft	aft	aft		aft	aft
	Shrewsbury (Gen.)..dep.	....	Mondays only.	....	8 10	....	1125	1 10	Saturdays only.	Except Saturdays.		5 30	7 50	....
4½	Berrington	....		....	8 22	....	1135	1 20				5 40	7 59	....
8¼	Cressage	....		....	8 32	....	1143	1 28				5 47	8 6	....
12¼	Buildwas 94	....		....	8 50	....	1153	1 37				5 57	8 14	....
13¾	Iron Bridge and Broseley	....		....	8 57	....	12 0	1 43				6 7	8 20	....
15¾	Coalport 446	....		....	9 2	....	12 5	1 48				6 12	8 25	....
18¼	Linley	....		....	9 8	....	1211	1 54				6 18	....	....
22½	Bridgnorth ...... arr.	....		....	9 15	....	1218	2 1				6 25	8 37	m
	dep.	....	7 0	....	9 20	....	1221	....	2 15	2 45		6 35	8 42	9 5
24¾	Eardington........	....	....	....	9 28	....	1227	....	2 21	2 52		6 41	....	....
27	Hampton Loade........	m	7 10	....	9 35	....	1232	....	2 30	2 58		6 48	8 53	9 16
29¼	Highley	6 5	7 16	....	9 43	....	1238	....	2 36	3 4		6 54	8 59	9 23
31½	Arley	6 15	7 22	....	9 50	....	1244	....	2 42	3 10		7 2	9 5	9 30
35¼	Bewdley 90, 99....arr.	6 22	7 29	....	9 57	....	1251	....	2 49	3 17		7 9	9 12	9 38
38¾	90 KIDDERMINSTR 96 ar.	6 45	7 41	....	10 8	....	1 8	....	3 0	3 29	7 25	....	9 22	9 50
57¾	96 BIRMINGHAM(S.H.) "	8 33	8 40	....	11 12	....	2 35	....	4 25	4 25	8 25	....	10 30	11 12
—	Bewdley ....dep.	....	....	7n45	....	11n0	1 0	....	3 10	3 22	....	7n13	....	....
37½	Stourport........	....	....	7n55	....	11n8	1 8	....	3 18	3 30	....	7n19	....	....
40¾	Hartlebury 96 ... arr.	....	....	8n1	....	1115	1 15	....	3 25	3 37	....	7n26	....	....
	dep.	....	....	8 17	....	1123	1 30	....	3 47	3 47	....	8 13	10c4	10c4
46½	Droitwich 630........	....	....	8 28	10c52	1135	1 41	....	3 58	3 58	8c8	8 25	10c15	10c15
49½	Fernhill Heath[106,626	....	....	8 37	....	1144	....	....	4 5	4 5	....	8 32	....	....
52	Worcester * 95,100, arr.	....	....	8 45	11B2	1150	1 50	....	4 11	4 11	8B18	8 40	10c25	10c25

a Departure time.
B Worcester (Foregate Street), via Kidderminster.
c Via Kidderminster.
m Motor Car, one class only.
n Motor Car, one class only.
R Arrives Buildwas at 8 50 mrn.
* Shrub Hill.
† General Station; about ½ mile to Abbey Station (S. & M.).

WORCESTER, BEWDLEY, BRIDGNORTH, BUILDWAS, and SHREWSBURY.

Miles	Down.	Week Days only. mrn N	mrn N	mrn	mrn N	mrn	mrn N		aft	aft N	aft Z	aft N	
—	(Shrub Hill) Worcester ¶ ...... dep.	..	..	7 2	..	..		..	1 25	..	5 25	..	..
2½	Fernhill Heath	..	..	7 9	..	..		..	1 31	..	5 31	..	..
5½	Droitwich Spa	..	..	7 17	..	..	Sats. only.	..	1 38	..	5 38	..	..
9	Cutnall Green	..	..	..	..	..		..	..	..	5 44	..	..
11½	Hartlebury	..	..	7 29	..	..		..	2 A15	..	6 B3	..	..
14½	Stourport-on-Severn ¶ ..	..	..	7 36	..	..		..	2 24	..	6 12	..	..
16½	**Bewdley 134, 138** .. arr.	..	..	7 43	..	..		..	2 31	..	6 19	..	..
—	120 BIRMINGHM (S. H) dep	..	5 40	6 15	8 7	8 55	1030	..	1 0	2 18	5 0	7 10	..
—	138 KIDDERMINSTER. "	5 40	6 50	7 39	9 45	1050	1240	..	2 10	3 45	5 48	8 12	..
—	**Bewdley ¶** .... dep.	5 50	7 2	7 53	9 58	11 0	1252	..	2 34	3 54	6 23	8 27	..
20½	Arley	6 0	7 9	8 0	10 5	11 7	1 0	..	2 44	4 1	6 30	8 35	..
22¾	Highley	6 6	7 14	8 6	1011	1114	1 6	..	2 47	4 8	6 36	8 41	..
25	Hampton Loade	..	..	8 12	1018	1121	..	..	2 54	4 14	6 44	8 47	..
27¼	Eardington	..	..	8 17	1024	1126	..	..	3 0	4 19	6 50	Yy	..
29½	**Bridgnorth** ...... arr.	..	..	8 22	1028	1130	..	..	3 5	4 23	6 55	8 56	..
	dep.	..	..	8 28	..	1135	..	..	3 9	..	7 0	..	..
33¾	Linley	..	..	8 36	..	1144	..	..	3 17	..	7 8	..	..
36¼	Coalport **H** ¶ 484	..	..	8 41	..	1151	..	..	3 23	..	7 14	..	..
38¼	Iron Bridge and Broseley	..	..	8 48	..	12 2	..	..	3 32	..	7 22	..	..
39¾	Buildwas 138	..	..	8 55	..	1212	..	..	3 40	..	7 30	..	..
43¾	Cressage ¶ .... [492	..	..	9 2	..	1218	..	..	3 46	..	7 36	..	..
47¾	Berrington ... [488, 490,	..	..	9 12	..	1232	..	..	3 56	..	7 46	..	..
52	**Shrewsbury G 108**, arr.	..	..	9 22	..	1243	..	..	4 7	..	7 57	..	..

Miles	Up.	Week Days only. mrn N	mrn N	mrn	mrn N		non	aft N	aft	aft N	aft N	aft	aft N	aft Z
—	**Shrewsbury** (Gen.) .. dep.	..	..	8 15	..	..	12 0	..	..	..	..	5 30	..	8 30
4¼	Berrington ¶	..	..	8 26	..	..	1210	..		..	..	5 40	..	8 40
8¼	Cressage	..	..	8 37	..	..	1220	..		..	..	5 50	..	8 50
12¼	Buildwas 138	..	..	8 54	..	..	1230	..	Saturdays only.	..	..	5 58	..	8 59
13¾	Iron Bridge & Broseley ¶	..	..	9 1	..	..	1238	..		..	..	6 7	..	9 5
15¾	Coalport **H** 484	..	..	9 8	..	..	1245	..		..	..	6 15	..	9 14
18¼	Linley	..	..	9 13	..	..	1251	..		..	..	6 21	..	9 20
22½	**Bridgnorth** ...... arr.	..	..	9 20	..	..	1258	..		..	..	6 28	..	9 27
	dep.	..	..	9 26	1220	..	1 3	..		..	4 35	6 32	9 10	9 31
24¾	Eardington	..	..	9 31	1225	..	1 8	..		..	4 40	6 37	Zz	..
27	Hampton Loade	..	..	9 36	1231	..	1 13	..		..	4 45	6 44	9 20	9 41
29¼	Highley	6 15	7 17	9 42	1239	..	1 20	..	2 0	3 15	4 51	6 50	9 26	9 48
31¼	Arley ¶	6 21	7 22	9 48	1246	..	1 26	..	2 6	3 21	4 57	6 56	9 32	9 54
35¼	**Bewdley 134, 138** . arr.	6 27	7 28	9 56	1257	..	1 34	..	2 14	3 29	5 5	7 5	9 40	10 0
38¾	139 KIDDERMINSTER arr.	6 40	7 39	10 6	1 10	..	..	..	2 29	3 39	5 15	7 15	9 50	..
57¾	118 BIRMINGHM (S.H.) "	8 5	8 40	11 11	2 27	..	..	..	3 36	5 5	6 25	9 5	..	..
—	**Bewdley ¶** .... dep.	..	..	..	1 0	..	1 37	..	..	..	..	..	..	10 2
37¾	Stourport-on-Severn	..	..	..	1 10	..	1 47	..	..	..	..	..	..	1012
40½	**Hartlebury 118**	..	..	..	1 C17	..	1 55	2 55	..	..	..	..	..	1020
43	Cutnall Green	..	..	..	..	..	..	3 0	..	..	..	..	..	..
46½	Droitwich Spa **660**	..	..	..	1 45	..	..	3 8	..	..	..	..	..	1033
49½	Fernhill H'th ¶ **656** ...	..	..	..	..	..	..	3 14	..	..	..	..	..	..
52	**Worcester F 117, 122** ar.	..	..	..	1 55	..	..	3 21	..	..	..	..	..	1045

A Arr. 1 52 aft. B Arr. 5 53 aft. C Arr. 1 33 aft. F Shrub Hill. G General. H About 200 yards to L.M.&S. Station. N Third class only (limited accommodation). Yy Stops to set down on notice to Guard at Hampton Loade. Z Does not call at Cound Halt during the hours of darkness. Zz Stops to set down on notice to Guard at Bridgnorth.

¶ "Halts" at Astwood, between Worcester (S.H.) and Fernhill Heath; at Burlish, between Stourport-on-Severn and Bewdley; at Northwood between Bewdley and Arley; at Jackfield, between Coalport and Iron Bridge and Broseley; and at Cound, between Cressage and Berrington.

February 1942

SPECIAL DAY EXCURSION TICKETS

— TO —

ARLEY, HIGHLEY, HAMPTON LOADE and BRIDGNORTH

MONDAY, 10th JUNE

FROM	DEPARTURE TIMES "A"	"B"	RETURN FARES—SECOND CLASS Arley	Highley	Hampton Loade	Bridg-north
	a.m.	a.m.	s. d.	s. d.	s. d.	s. d.
Birmingham (Snow Hill)	9 15	10 30	4/6	5/–	5/2	5/10
Hockley	9 18	10 33	4/6	5/–	5/2	5/10
Soho & W. G.	9 21	10 36	4/6	5/–	5/2	5/10
Handsworth & S.	9 25	10 40	4/3	4/9	4/11	5/7
Smethwick West	9 30	10 45	4/–	4/6	4/8	5/4
Oldbury & L.G.	9 34	10 49	3/9	4/3	4/5	5/1
Rowley Regis & B.	9 38	10 53	3/6	4/–	4/2	4/10
Old Hill	9 42	10 57	3/4	3/10	4/–	4/8
Cradley Heath & C.	9 47	11 2	3/2	3/8	3/10	4/6
Lye	9 51	11 6	3/1	3/7	3/9	4/5
Wolverhampton (Low Level)		9C 50	4/9	5/3	5/5	6/1
Priestfield		9C 55	4/6	5/–	5/2	5/10
Bilston (West)	Change	9C 59	4/6	5/–	5/2	5/10
Daisy Bank & B.		10C 3	4/3	4/9	4/11	5/7
Princes End & C.	at	10C 7	4/–	4/6	4/8	5/4
Tipton (Five Ways)		10C 11	3/9	4/3	4/5	5/1
Dudley	Kidder-	10C 18	3/8	4/2	4/4	5/–
Blowers Green		10C 20	3/4	3/10	4/–	4/8
Round Oak	minster	10C 27	3/4	3/10	4/–	4/8
Brierley Hill		10C 30	3/2	3/8	3/10	4/6
Brettell Lane		10C 33	3/1	3/7	3/9	4/5
Stourbridge Town	9C 35	11C 5	3/–	3/6	3/8	4/4
Stourbridge Junction	10 2	11 15	2/10	3/4	3/6	4/2
ARRIVAL TIMES	"A"		a.m. 11 0	a.m. 11 6	a.m. 11 12	a.m. 11 22
	"B"		a.m. 11 55	p.m. 12 2	p.m. 12 10	p.m. 12 22

NOTE

C—CHANGE AT STOURBRIDGE JUNCTION.

SPL.D.

PASSENGERS RETURN ON DAY OF OUTWARD JOURNEY BY ANY TRAIN AFFORDING A SERVICE THROUGH TO DESTINATION.

NOTICE AS TO CONDITIONS

These tickets are issued subject to the British Transport Commission's published Regulations and Conditions applicable to British Railways exhibited at their Stations or obtainable free of charge at station booking Offices.

TICKETS CAN BE OBTAINED IN ADVANCE AT BOOKING STATIONS AND AGENCIES

Further information will be supplied on application to Stations, Official Railway Agents, or to Mr. D. S. HART, District Passenger Manager, New Street Station, Birmingham 2 (Telephone Central 5071—Extension "Enquiries") or Mr. A. C. B. PICKFORD, Chief Commercial Manager, Paddington Station, W.2.

Paddington Station,
May, 1957.

K. W. C. GRAND,
General Manager.

B.H.58

Printed in England by Joseph Wones Ltd., West Bromwich; also Birmingham and London

Whitsuntide 1957.
(D.A.Johnson coll.)

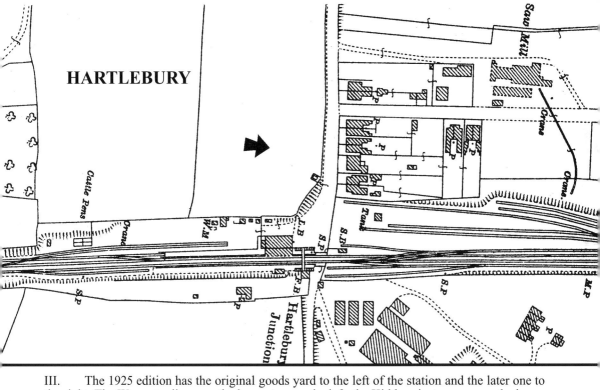

HARTLEBURY

III.   The 1925 edition has the original goods yard to the left of the station and the later one to the right. The Worcester lines are the lower two on the left, the Kidderminster ones are the lower two on the right and the single line to the Severn Valley is above them. Branching from it was a sand siding (1917-67) and one to a fuel depot (1941-64).

1.   A northward view in 1963 includes the unusual four-flight footbridge and the novel waiting room on the up side. These features have gone, but the other buildings were still standing in 2007 and the signal box was still in use, although with a panel since 1982.
(P.J.Garland/R.S.Carpenter coll.)

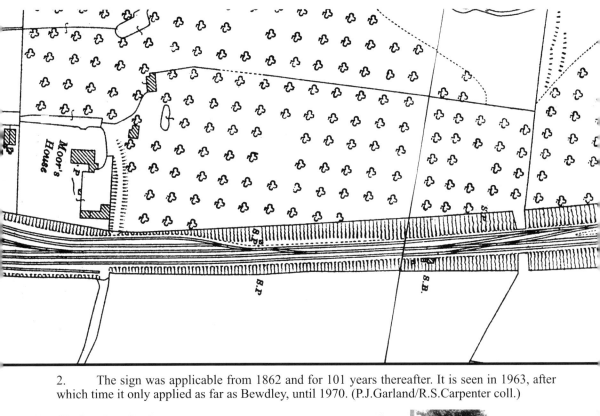

Moor's House

2.   The sign was applicable from 1862 and for 101 years thereafter. It is seen in 1963, after which time it only applied as far as Bewdley, until 1970. (P.J.Garland/R.S.Carpenter coll.)

3.   Seen in 1964 as a 4100 class 2-6-2T approaches, the goods yard closed on 1st February 1965. Beyond the six-ton crane are the cattle pens. (D.Johnson)

> **Other views of this station can be
> seen in pictures 23-27 in our
> *Worcester to Birmingham* album.**

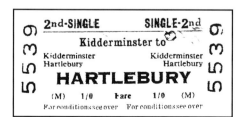

2nd-SINGLE   SINGLE-2nd
5539
Kidderminster to
Kidderminster   Kidderminster
Hartlebury   Hartlebury
HARTLEBURY
(M)   1/0   Fare   1/0   (M)
For conditions see over   For conditions see over

Great Western Railway
Ticket for Perambulator or Childs Mail Car
accompanying a Passenger
509
KIDDERMINSTER TO
any Station
not exceeding   100 miles
CARRIAGE PAID 5/11 Z
This ticket is available for a single journey
only & must be given up at destination Station

EAST OF STOURPORT

4.   Two sidings for the massive Stourport Power Station came into use on 7th May 1941 and this 1963 view is of the southern end of the system. A further five sidings were laid (in 1944 and 1960), but coal traffic ceased in March 1979. Line closure was on 12th January 1981, the track being in place as far as Stourport level crossing. (J.H.Moss/R.S.Carpenter coll.)

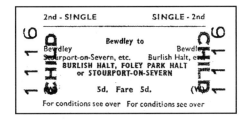

STOURPORT-ON-SEVERN

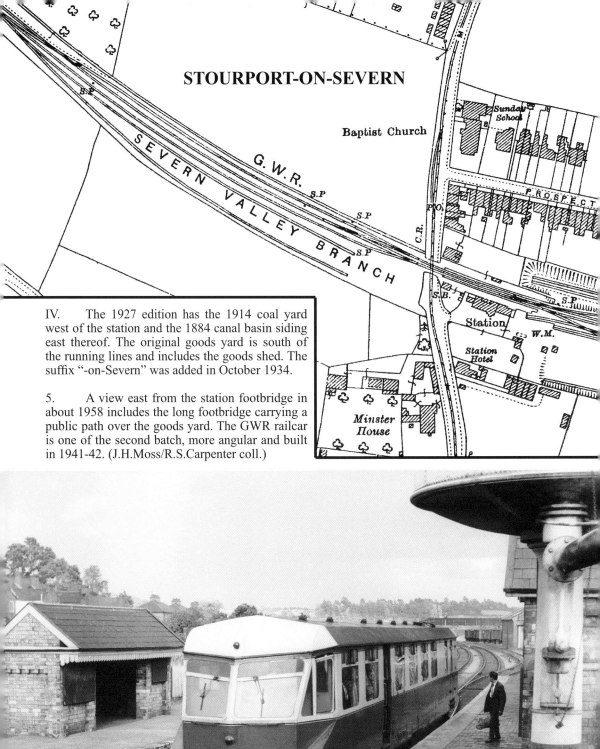

Baptist Church

G.W.R.

SEVERN VALLEY BRANCH

Sunday School

PROSPECT

P.O.

Station

Station Hotel

Minster House

IV.   The 1927 edition has the 1914 coal yard west of the station and the 1884 canal basin siding east thereof. The original goods yard is south of the running lines and includes the goods shed. The suffix "-on-Severn" was added in October 1934.

5.   A view east from the station footbridge in about 1958 includes the long footbridge carrying a public path over the goods yard. The GWR railcar is one of the second batch, more angular and built in 1941-42. (J.H.Moss/R.S.Carpenter coll.)

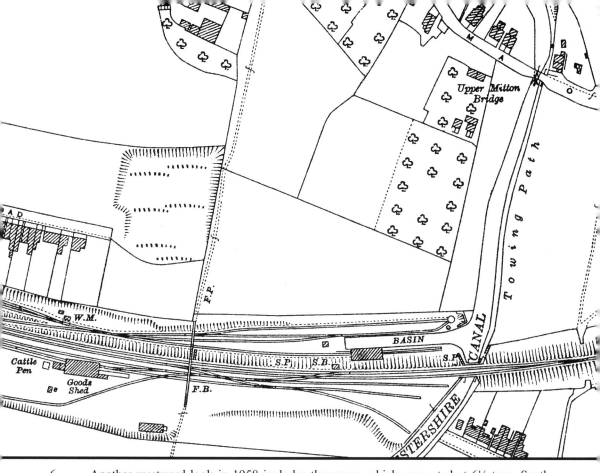

Upper Milton Bridge

Towing Path

CANAL

BASIN

S.P. S.B. S.P.

A D

W.M.

Cattle Pen

Goods Shed

F.B.

F.P.

...STERSHIRE

6.   Another westward look in 1958 includes the crane, which was rated at 6½ tons. South signal box had been in the distance until April 1951. In the right foreground is the weighbridge. (J.H.Moss/R.S.Carpenter coll.)

7.   The 3.53pm from Shrewsbury is arriving behind 2-6-2T no. 82005 on 29th April 1961. In the background are the silo and emergency food store for which sidings were provided in 1941. The loco is on the A451 and the line on the left formed the goods loop. From it was a private siding for Steatite & Porcelain Products Ltd. (D.Johnson)

8.   The goods yard closed on 1st February 1965 and this DMU was recorded on the last day of passenger service, 3rd January 1970. The 43-lever signal box ("North" until 1951) lasted until 3rd May 1970, having opened in 1885. There is now no trace of the station or even the church. The south elevation of the main building was similar to that still to be seen at Bewdley, although there were two flat-roofed additions. (D.Johnson)

BURLISH HALT

9.   The halt opened on 31st March 1930 and is seen in 1958 with the silo from picture 7 in the background. The siding described at the end of that caption curves behind the signal post, which carries Bewdley South distant. (Stations UK)

10.   North of the halt was the 123yd long Mount Pleasant Tunnel, which was cut through Sandstone. This is the south end of it in 1960 and included is Stourport's distant signal. (D.Ibbotson/R.S.Carpenter coll.)

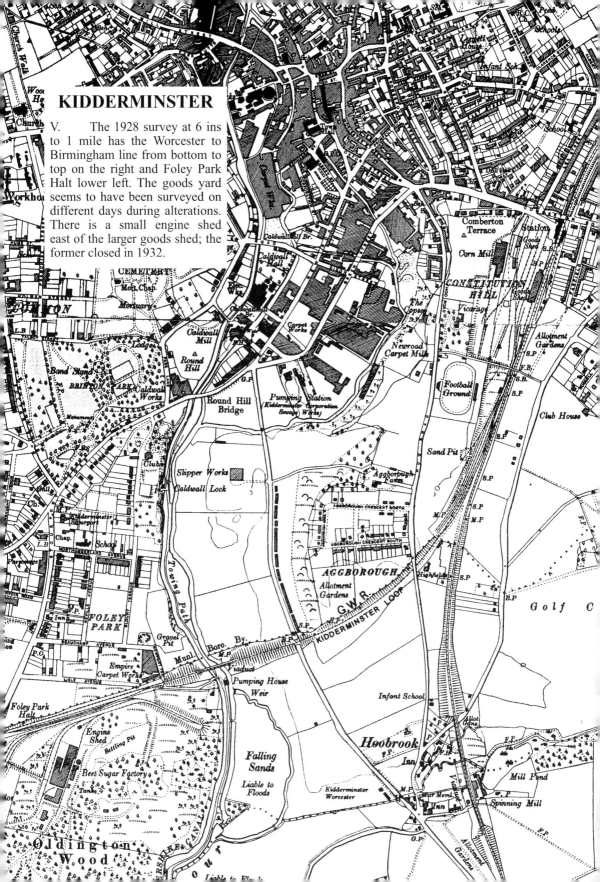

KIDDERMINSTER

V.   The 1928 survey at 6 ins
to 1 mile has the Worcester to
Birmingham line from bottom to
top on the right and Foley Park
Halt lower left. The goods yard
seems to have been surveyed on
different days during alterations.
There is a small engine shed
east of the larger goods shed; the
former closed in 1932.

11.　　The driver of a southbound 2-4-0 looks back, as youngsters gaze at it. The ventilated van is adjacent to Kidderminster Station Signal Box, which was in use until 15th July 1973. (Chambers coll./HMRS)

12.　　This was the third station building on the site, the first lasting until 1859 and the second until 1863. Seen in the late 1950s, decay set in to the elegant structure and it had to be demolished in 1968. (R.S.Carpenter)

13.   A panorama from the footbridge shown on the map features no. 6849 *Walton Grange* accelerating the 4.55pm Stourbridge Junction to Worcester Shrub Hill stopping train on 27th April 1964. The larger goods shed is behind the train. (P.Chancellor)

14.   The new platform was the only permanent structure when SVR traffic commenced here in July 1984. The GWR-style buildings came into use in September 1985 and are seen in 1989. (H.P.White/A.C.Mott coll.)

15.   The connection with BR (right) was restored in December 1984 and no. 7325 of the GWR 4300 class is seen departing for Bridgnorth on 17th April 1993. The new Kidderminster Station Signal Box (centre) came into use in 1986, it being equipped with a 62-lever frame. The goods shed behind it became the SVR's carriage repair shop in 1985 and the smaller shed (left) houses the splendid Kidderminster Railway Museum. (T.Heavyside)

16.   The new station was based on the plan used by the GWR at Ross-on-Wye and was photographed on 23rd July 2006. The ornate ironwork was a late addition. (V.Mitchell)

17.   Seen on the same day, the concourse was nearing completion, the roof being yet another commendable feature on the amazing SVR. A traditional buffet and booking hall have also been carefully recreated. (V.Mitchell)

> **Further details of the main line station can be found in captions 33-41 in our *Worcester to Birmingham* album.**

SOUTH OF KIDDERMINSTER

18.   Looking south from the same viewpoint as picture 13, we see 0-6-0PT no. 9646 working in the extensive sidings, beyond which is the curve to Bewdley. The down main line is on the left; the SVR now runs across the middle of the picture. (P.Chancellor)

19.   The engine shed did not open until 1932 and is thus not shown on the map. It was built below the word LOOP and was the base for about 20 locomotives, mostly tank engines. The usual murk prevailed when nos 8105 and 4114 were recorded in 1960. (D.K.Jones coll.)

20.   The elevated coaling stage is behind no. 29, seen on 21st November 1948. The loco was ex-Cleobury Mortimer & Ditton Priors Railway. The BR shed code was 85D and closure came on 10th August 1964. (D.K.Jones coll.)

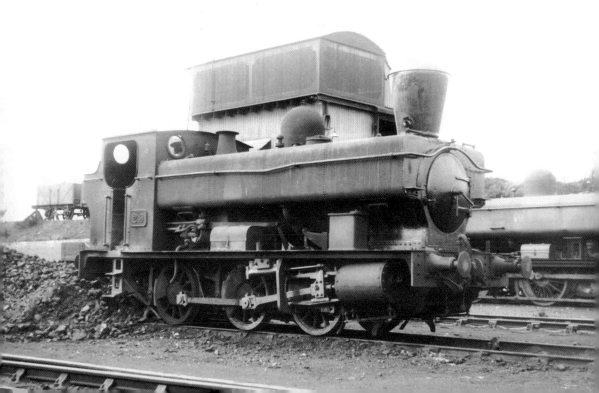

21. Carriage sheds are lacking on so many private railways, but the SVR built the biggest. It is west of the running line and is seen nearing completion on 23rd January 2000. It was built near the site of Kidderminster Junction. (P.Chancellor)

22. The 1937 box was demolished due to a derailment and this replacement came into use on 25th October 1953. It has a 66-lever frame and is still in use. (J.G.S.Smith)

FOLEY PARK HALT

23.   The location is lower left on the last map, as is the sugar beet factory, the headshunt for which is on the left of this view towards Bewdley. The halt was opened on 2nd January 1905 and was on the other side of the track until 1925. (Lens of Sutton coll.)

24.   Looking in the other direction in 1966, we have the seasonally used sidings for sugar beet traffic on the right. Fields Sand Siding was on the left, in the distance, between about 1901 and 1923. Beyond it is Kidderminster Viaduct, which is 132 yds in length. It is also known as Falling Sands Viaduct. (Stations UK)

25.   The use of beet for sugar began in the UK in 1912 and there were 18 factories by 1936, largely supplied by rail. The sidings here for the West Midland Sugar Co. Ltd. came into use on 27th May 1925. The works was part of the British Sugar Corporation from 1937, but rail traffic ceased here in June 1983. The works closed completely in 2002. Andrew Barclay 0-4-0ST no. 3 of 1948 is seen at work on 3rd December 1948. (M.A.N.Johnston)

SOUTH OF BEWDLEY

26.　　　The line passes through a ridge of Sandstone between the Stour and Severn Valleys in Bewdley Tunnel, which is 486 yds in length. Emerging from its west end on 17th April 1977 is class 4MT 2-6-4T no. 80079 working a special train. Rifle Range Halt was west of the tunnel, on the north side of the line, from 1905 to 1920. (T.Heavyside)

27.   The stock on the left is stored on the remains of the line from Hartlebury and Stourport. No. 43106 is working a special train as far as Foley Park on 12th September 1977 to view the unopened part of the SVR. No. 45110 is attached to the rear, to pull it back. Animals from around the world are kept in the West Midland Safari Park, behind the fence. (T.Heavyside)

28.   The Kidderminster and Hartlebury lines had run as two single tracks over Sandbourne Viaduct (101 yds), converging at the south end of it. A new bridge to pass over the Bewdley bypass opened in November 1986, near the south end of the viaduct. (T.Heavyside)

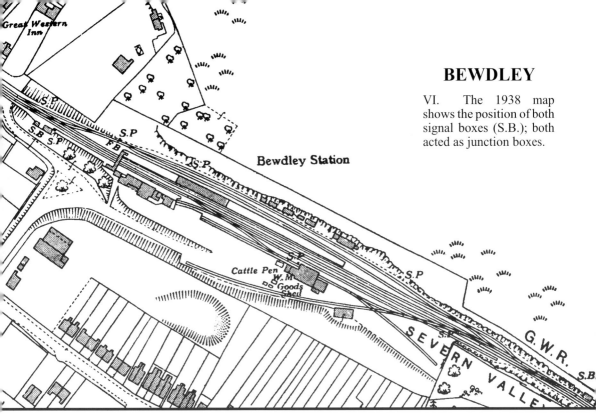

BEWDLEY

VI. The 1938 map shows the position of both signal boxes (S.B.); both acted as junction boxes.

Bewdley Station

29.   Railmotor no. 91 is smoking as it awaits reversal on its journey between Kidderminster and Stourport. Centre is an LNWR coach with roof boards stating THROUGH CARRIAGE BETWEEN BIRMINGHAM AND WOOFFERTON VIA SMETHWICK. The scene is about 1910. The through service ceased with World War I. (Lens of Sutton coll.)

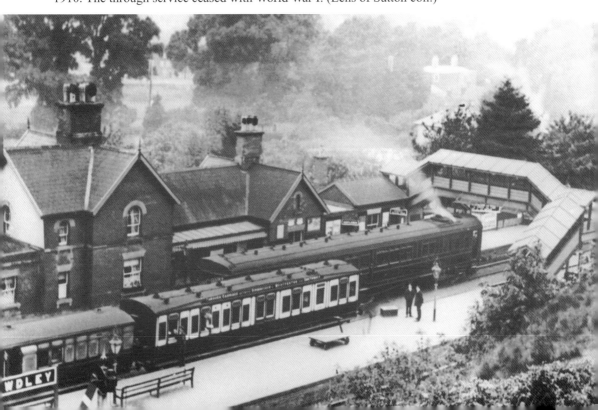

30.   When the station first became a junction, it was provided with a lengthy island platform, in addition to the short one next to the entrance. This Edwardian view includes oil lit coaches. (Chambers coll./HMRS)

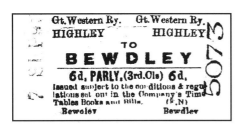

31.   From the same era, we have the classic display of staff, a horse-drawn taxi, a horsebox and Bewdley North signal box, together with the junction signals for the branch to Cleobury Mortimer and Woofferton. (Kidderminster Railway Museum)

32.   Seen on 2nd October 1954 is 5100 class 2-6-2T no. 4103 running in with the 4.23pm Kidderminster to Shrewsbury. On the left is a Bewdley to Hartlebury service. South box is in the distance; it had 32 levers. (T.J.Edgington)

33. Class 5700 0-6-0PT no. 4641 is about to leave with the 4.20pm Shrewsbury to Kidderminster on 14th September 1956. At the change of platform level is a cast iron urinal, still a feature at this location, although now one rescued and restored, from Melrose on the Waverley route. (R.M.Casserley)

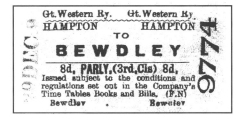

Gt. Western Ry.   Gt. Western Ry.
HAMPTON   HAMPTON
TO
BEWDLEY
8d, PARLY.(3rd.Cls) 8d,
Issued subject to the conditions and regulations set out in the Company's Time Tables Books and Bills. (F.N)
Bewdley . Bewdley
9774

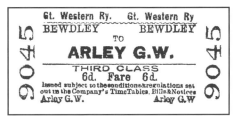

Gt. Western Ry.   Gt. Western Ry
BEWDLEY   BEWDLEY
TO
ARLEY G.W.
THIRD CLASS
6d.   Fare   6d.
Issued subject to the conditions&regulations set out in the Company's TimeTables, Bills&Notices
Arley G.W.   Arley G.W
9045

34.   The cramped goods yard (right) had closed on 1st February 1965. It was used for coach restoration when this photograph was taken in June 1979. A paint shop was erected at the far end of it. (F.Hornby)

35.   Running in from Bridgnorth on 21st August 1977 is ex-LMS class 8F 2-8-0 no. 8235. The train is on Bewdley Viaduct. North box has 37 levers; both were closed in May 1970 and both are in use again. (M.Turvey)

NORTH OF BEWDLEY

36.   No. 46443 was renumbered 60116 and disguised for Universal Pictures *Seven per cent Solution* filming purposes. It is running north on 19th May 1976, parallel to the trackbed of the Woofferton line, which soon curved away westwards. (T.Heavyside)

VIa. The 1 ins to 1 mile map from 1946 shows both Burlish Halt and Northwood Halt.

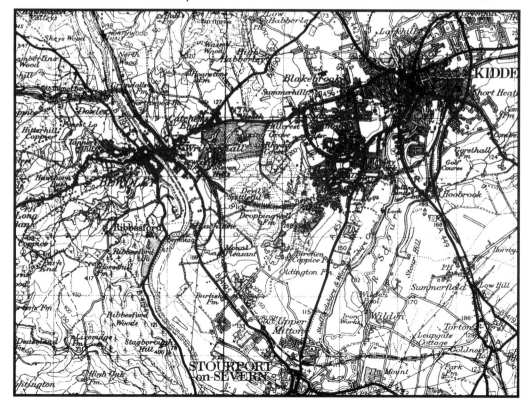

NORTHWOOD HALT

37. The halt opened on 17th June 1935 and can be seen to be on the side of the valley. Class 3 2-6-2T no. 82005 is about to stop at 3.36pm on 29th April 1961, on its way to Hartlebury. (D.Johnson)

38. A hand signalman stands on the unprotected level crossing by the third coach. No. 193 is a Hunslet Austerity 0-6-0ST of 1953 and is working the 13.15 from Bewdley on 16th May 1976. There are now lights and audible warning of approaching trains. (T.Heavyside)

39.   Passing over the River Severn on 12th September 1976 is no. 46521 with a train for Bridgnorth. The Victoria Bridge foundation stone was laid by Mr. Bridgeman and following renovation in 2004 the bridge was reopened by Miss Victoria Bridge. Neither lived in Bridgnorth. (T.Heavyside)

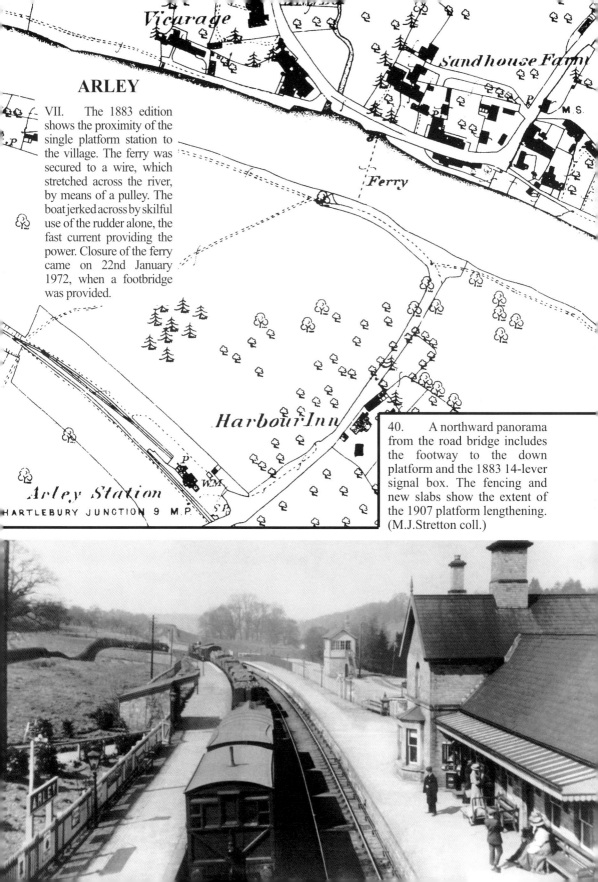

ARLEY

VII. The 1883 edition shows the proximity of the single platform station to the village. The ferry was secured to a wire, which stretched across the river, by means of a pulley. The boat jerked across by skilful use of the rudder alone, the fast current providing the power. Closure of the ferry came on 22nd January 1972, when a footbridge was provided.

Vicarage

Sandhouse Farm

Ferry

Harbour Inn

Arley Station

HARTLEBURY JUNCTION 9 M.P.

40. A northward panorama from the road bridge includes the footway to the down platform and the 1883 14-lever signal box. The fencing and new slabs show the extent of the 1907 platform lengthening. (M.J.Stretton coll.)

41.   A view east across the valley includes the lamp room (left) and weighbridge office, beyond the ARLEY sign. This postcard was produced prior to 1907. (B.Geens coll.)

VIII.   The 1927 map reveals the extent of the 1883 passing loop and the position of the signal box. An additional siding has been laid behind it, since preservation.

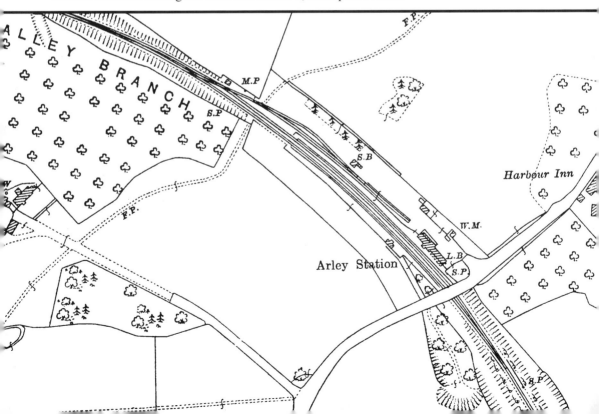

42.   A camp coach was provided here (and at Hampton Loade) for the Summer of 1938 only. It had six berths and was available for £3 per week, but water had to be carried, both fresh and soiled. All other railways used the term camping coach. (J.Speight)

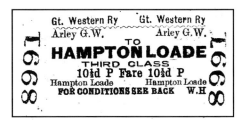

43.	Sighting of the up starting signal had been improved since picture 41 was taken. This one is from 1954 and the railcar is probably no. 9. The signal box closed on 28th June 1964, when there ceased to be a loop. Both passenger and freight services ended on 9th September 1963. (SLS coll.)

44.	One track was retained for coal traffic, but everything else was neglected or destroyed. This is 1971 and even the down platform has largely vanished. Only a few bricks of the signal box base remained, out of sight. (P.J.G.Ransom)

45.   We move forward to 7th September 1980 and the enterprising SVR was able to offer photographers an authentic mixed freight behind no. 5764. The box had been rebuilt to a high standard using the LNWR structure from Yorton (near Wem), into which the 30-lever frame from Kidderminster Station box was installed. It was in use from 10th April 1976. (T.Heavyside)

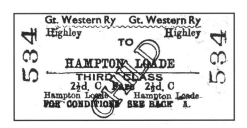

Gt. Western Ry   Gt. Western Ry
Highley   Highley
534   TO   534
HAMPTON LOADE
THIRD CLASS
2½d. C   FARE   2½d. C
Hampton Loade   Hampton Loade
FOR CONDITIONS SEE BACK A.

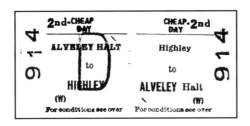

46.   Like most heritage railways, the line has an excess of rolling stock awaiting restoration. However, the quality of the operational fleet is outstanding, as could be witnessed on 16th April 1994 as ex-LMS "Jubilee" no. 45596 *Bahamas* arrives. (M.Turvey)

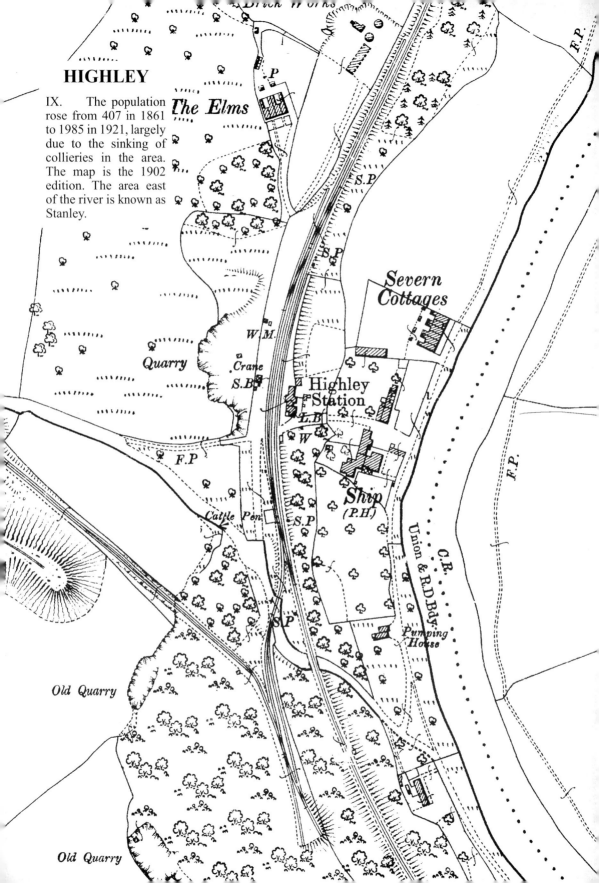

HIGHLEY

IX.   The population rose from 407 in 1861 to 1985 in 1921, largely due to the sinking of collieries in the area. The map is the 1902 edition. The area east of the river is known as Stanley.

The Elms

Severn Cottages

S.P.

Quarry

Crane
S.B.

W.M.

Highley Station

L.B.

W

F.P.

Cattle Pen

S.P.

S.P.

Ship
(P.H.)

C.R.
Union & R.D.Bdy.

Pumping House

S.P

Old Quarry

Old Quarry

F.P.

47.   An ex-GWR railcar is passing the disused cattle dock, sometime in the 1950s. South of the station, there were branches on the west side of the line to Billingsley Colliery (to 1921) and Kinlet Colliery (to 1935). They were controlled by the 38-lever Kinlet signal box, which was in use from about 1913 to 1943. (Lens of Sutton coll.)

48.   The station changed little and was recorded from the footbridge on 17th April 1959. The white paint was applied to the stonework as an aid during the wartime blackout. Much extra freight traffic was conveyed on the route during that period. (R.M.Casserley)

49.   Coal from the local colliery is seen on the same day. The footbridge was demolished shortly before the station reopened, owing to corrosion. The signal box is partially visible. (R.M.Casserley)

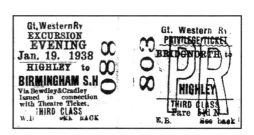

50. A BR railcar from Bewdley passes the overgrown branch to Highley Colliery, which carried traffic from 1880 to 1940. A short siding was retained and was to be used again for The Engine House, which was under construction in 2007. On the left of this 1960s view are holiday homes of the type which abound between Bewdley and Hampton Loade. (D.Wilson)

51. The standard of restoration work, has brought awards and much praise. The signalman holds the staff high as class 4MT 2-6-0 no. 43106 runs in with the 13.30 from Bridgnorth on 18th August 1974. The fireman is offering a tablet in a pouch. (T.Heavyside)

52.   The 14-lever signal box survived the closure period intact, but the cattle pens were a reconstruction. Departing for Kidderminster on 9th May 1987 is "Peak" class no. D4 *Great Gable*. (D.H.Mitchell)

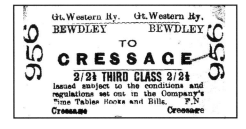

ALVELEY COLLIERY HALT

53. The Highley Mining Co. Ltd. sidings came into use on 30th January 1939 and were on the east side of the line. They were connected to the colliery by a ropeway across the river; there was also a bridge. (NRM)

54. The halt was provided for workers only and opened in about February 1944. Coal winding ceased on 31st March 1969 and the level crossing now serves a golf course. The view is towards Bridgnorth and is south of the sidings. (A.Dudman)

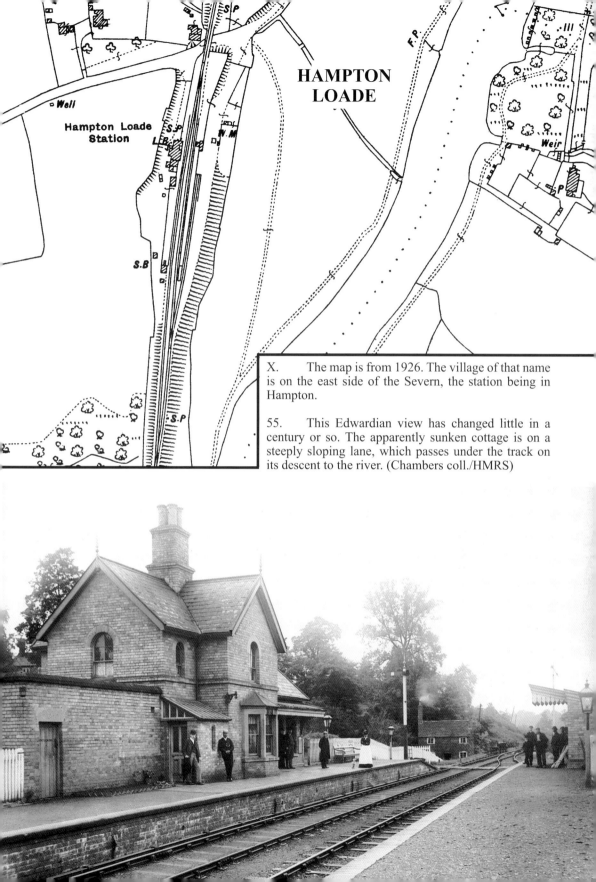

HAMPTON LOADE

Well

Hampton Loade
Station

S.B

X.	The map is from 1926. The village of that name is on the east side of the Severn, the station being in Hampton.

55.	This Edwardian view has changed little in a century or so. The apparently sunken cottage is on a steeply sloping lane, which passes under the track on its descent to the river. (Chambers coll./HMRS)

56.	No. 8718 is working to Kidderminster on 16th April 1954, as railcar no. W19W waits for the starting signal to proceed to Shrewsbury. Coal stands in the single siding. (T.J.Edgington)

57.	There was much still to be done on 1st September 1968 as no. 43106 terminated its journey. The signal box had lost its 14-lever frame, but a replacement was obtained from Ledbury North. (R.A.Lumber/D.H.Mitchell coll.)

58. Ex-LMS 0-6-0 no. 47383 is about to depart south on 17th April 1977, a replacement lamp room having been found by that time. The loop and signal box dated from 1883. Inside chaired track remained in the siding. No. 4141 is under restoration on the right. (T.Heavyside)

59.   Seen in August 1993, the ferry at the bottom of the lane provided students of transport history with a treat and others with a pleasant experience. The wire and one of the tethering posts can be seen on the left of the picture. (P.G.Barnes)

60.   Another magnificent restoration has been achieved at this station, as witnessed on 11th August 2006 while ex-LMS 4-6-0 no. 45110 *Biggin Hill* waits to cross a train from Bridgnorth. Passengers can cross the tracks on the level here. (V.Mitchell)

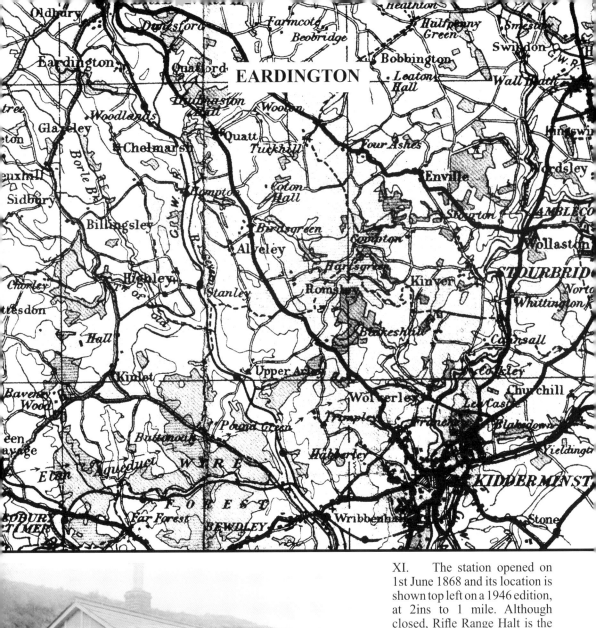

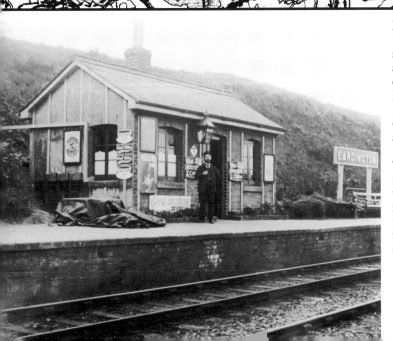

XI.   The station opened on 1st June 1868 and its location is shown top left on a 1946 edition, at 2ins to 1 mile. Although closed, Rifle Range Halt is the lowest station marked.

61.   The tiny station served a very small population (305 in 1901) and is seen in about 1910. The line in the foreground formed a goods loop until 1959, when the northern points were removed. There were two large forges nearby generating much traffic until about 1890.
(Stations UK)

62.   The goods yard saw little traffic and was in use by the engineers when photographed on 17th April 1959. It closed on 2nd December 1963. Staffing had ceased on 1st April 1949. (H.C.Casserley)

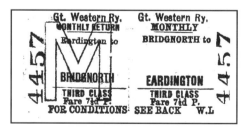

63.   With the reopening of the SVR, this was initially its only intermediate station and water source. It is seen on 1st September 1968, as ex-GWR 0-6-0 no. 3205 arrives from Bridgnorth. The water tank from Hampton-in-Arden was moved to Bridgnorth in September 1970. The one seen had come from Dudley, Windmill End. (R.A.Lumber/D.H.Mitchell coll.)

64.   The loop was reinstated and a dock was built mainly for the transfer of track materials. It was home for the steam crane for many years. No. 8233 is bound for Hampton Loade on 20th May 1973. Downgrading to a halt followed and closure came in 1982. (T.Heavyside)

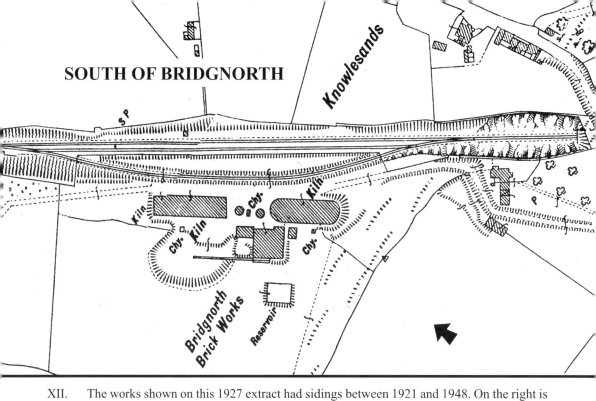

SOUTH OF BRIDGNORTH

Knowlesands

Kiln · *Chy.* *Kiln* · *Chy.* *Kiln*

Chy. *Kiln*

Chy.

Bridgnorth Brick Works

Reservoir

XII.   The works shown on this 1927 extract had sidings between 1921 and 1948. On the right is part of Knowle Sands Tunnel, which was only 40yds in length.

65.   Just beyond the left border of the map is Oldbury Viaduct, which is 87yds in length. We witness no. 8233 again, southbound on 16th April 1977. In the background is Daniels Mill; its 45ft diameter wheel was built by Abraham Darby. (T.Heavyside)

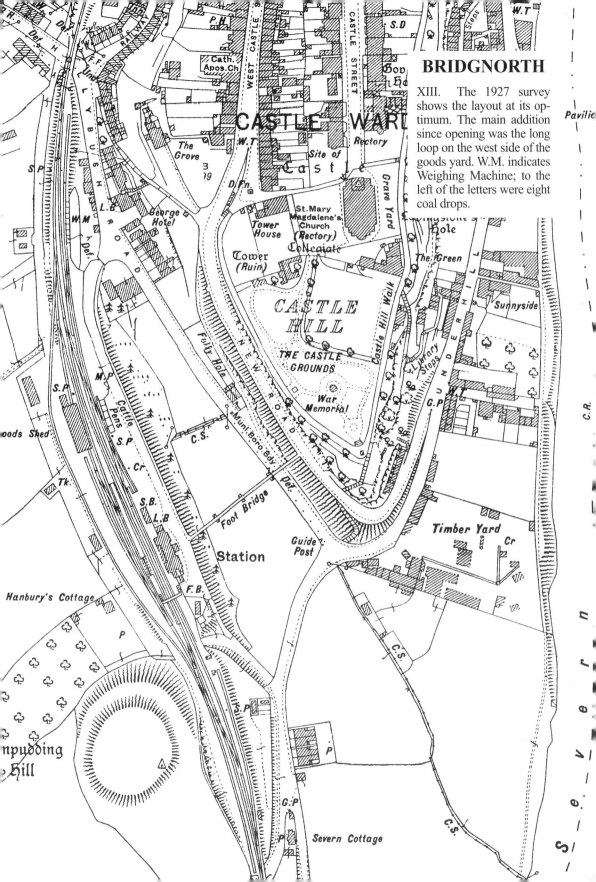

BRIDGNORTH

XIII. The 1927 survey shows the layout at its optimum. The main addition since opening was the long loop on the west side of the goods yard. W.M. indicates Weighing Machine; to the left of the letters were eight coal drops.

66. A northward panorama from Panpudding Hill in about 1900 has the castle ruins on the skyline, along with the church tower. Bridgnorth South box of 1892 is featured; it had 21 levers and closed in 1922. (J.Langford coll.)

67. The GWR pioneered connecting bus services and this is one of three Clarkson 20hp steam buses put into traffic between Bridgnorth and Wolverhampton on 7th November 1904. Their boilers proved troublesome and Milnes-Daimlers took over; these had petrol engines.
(Lens of Sutton coll.)

68.   No. 8718 was photographed near the cattle dock on 30th March 1955, with High Town in the background. The nearest wagon was for conveyance of cattle. (G.Adams/M.J.Stretton coll.)

69.   From the same location as no. 66, this panorama is from 17th April 1959 and includes class 2 2-6-2T no. 82004 with the 1.45pm Shrewsbury to Kidderminster. (R.M.Casserley)

70.　　The goods yard had a six-ton crane and closed on 1st December 1963. It is seen from the footbridge in about 1958; the new white building was for agricultural traffic. All the premises were leased from BR by the SVR in 1969. (J.Moss/R.S.Carpenter coll.)

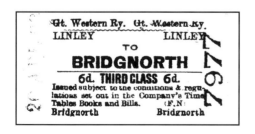

71.   The 1.45pm from Shrewsbury was hauled by ex-GWR 2-6-2T no. 5538 on 28th August 1961. The parcels and mailbags for the bewhiskered railcar will have been hauled over the crossing in the foreground. (H.B.Priestley/Ted Hancock)

72.   A northward view on the same day includes 2-6-2T no. 6128 near the cattle dock and no. W26 serving the Royal Mail. The 54-lever signal box replaced two in 1922 and was in use until 2nd December 1963. It was destroyed and later rebuilt by the SVR using the 30-lever frame from Windmill End Junction. (H.B.Priestley/Ted Hancock)

73.   This is the prospective passenger's perspective from New Road in 1963. The 1887 footbridge was closed in 1976 and its replacement was opened in 1994. There is also a cliff railway to the town, on its east side. It opened in 1892. (T.J.Edgington)

74.   Regular weekend trains to Hampton Loade did not begin until May 1970, but a service was operated on 1st September 1968 over that length, using nos 46443 (left) and 43106. The first stock had arrived on 25th March 1967. (R.A.Lumber/D.H.Mitchell coll.)

PASSENGE

75. The sectional warehouse was still present on 20th May 1973, as ex-LMS 2-8-0 no. 8233 of 1940 was coaled mechanically - no hydraulics in sight, or probably on site. The land was used for the massive engine shed in 1971 and it is seen in picture 78. (T.Heavyside)

76. As time passed, there was a growing interest in diesel traction and the SVR responded accordingly. By 2007, there were 17 listed, plus five DMU cars. No. D1013 *Western Ranger* of BR class 52 is about to depart on 8th July 1989. (P.G.Barnes)

77.   Ex-GWR 2-6-0 4300 class no. 7325 approaches the terminus on 17th April 1993. The proposed Bridgnorth Bypass threatened to sever the SVR in this vicinity for many years, but bridging eventually proved possible. (T.Heavyside)

78.   The spacious engine shed is seen on 2nd March 1996; beyond it is the old goods shed housing machine tools and beyond that is a new building for boiler work. Nearest are 2-6-2T no. 4566, 2-6-4T no. 80079 and 0-6-0T no. 47383. There were over 20 steam locos resident in 2007, plus five industrials. (M.J.Stretton)

79.   At the top of the last map is the south portal of High Town Tunnel (550 yds), seen here in April 1959. There was no space for the railway to be built between Low Town and the river, hence the tunnel. (D.Ibbotson/R.S.Carpenter coll.)

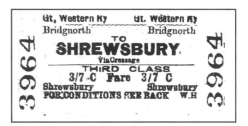

LINLEY

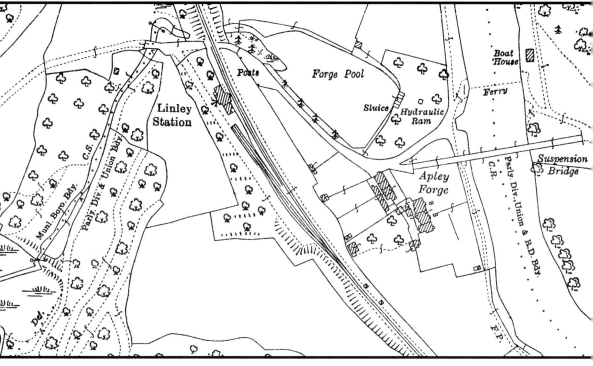

XIV.   The line ran close to the River Severn for many miles and its proximity is evident on this 1927 extract. The short goods loop was removed in about 1939.

80.   The local population was only 59 in 1901, but there was a forge nearby generating traffic. The small building in the centre of this postcard housed a ground frame.
(Kidderminster Railway Museum)

81.   No. 6128 was photographed shortly before total closure of this section in 1963. Staffing ceased, the term HALT was applied and the goods siding had closed on 10th September 1951. (P.C.Coutanche)

82.   A lone passenger leaves this northbound car as weeds begin to take over. The building is now a private house and the trackbed is used for a public footpath. (P.C.Coutanche)

COALPORT

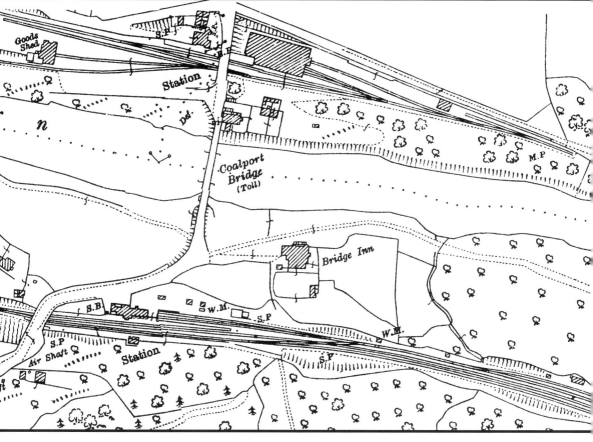

XV.   Our route is across the bottom of this 1927 extract and at the top is the terminus of the former LNWR 1861 branch from Hadley. The signal box (lower right) had 31 levers.

83.   Similar to other SVR stations, the entrance side of this one faced the river and the bridge over it. There were four employees here in the 1920s, but they handled little of the town's china output, this going on the competing route. (Lens of Sutton coll.)

84.   An action shot in the rain on 22nd September 1958 features no. 5355 on the reversible goods loop. The condemned wagons are on the line which once served the tile works. (H.C.Casserley)

85.   A northward panorama from the station in April 1959 has the former LNWR premises in the centre. The tallest building had been the engine shed. Part of the town is in the background. The cast iron bridge was completed in 1818 and was the third on the site since 1790. It was the last such bridge to carry vehicles. (H.C.Casserley)

Coalport	1903	1913	1923	1933
Passenger tickets issued	7906	6622	8974	5767
Season tickets issued	*	*	10	4
Parcels forwarded	1325	1257	1885	690
General goods forwarded (tons)	382	151	95	12
Coal and coke received (tons)	2009	1319	1747	1772
Other minerals received (tons)	353	214	30	149
General goods received (tons)	214	119	97	28
Trucks of livestock handled	11	15	8	4
(* not available)				

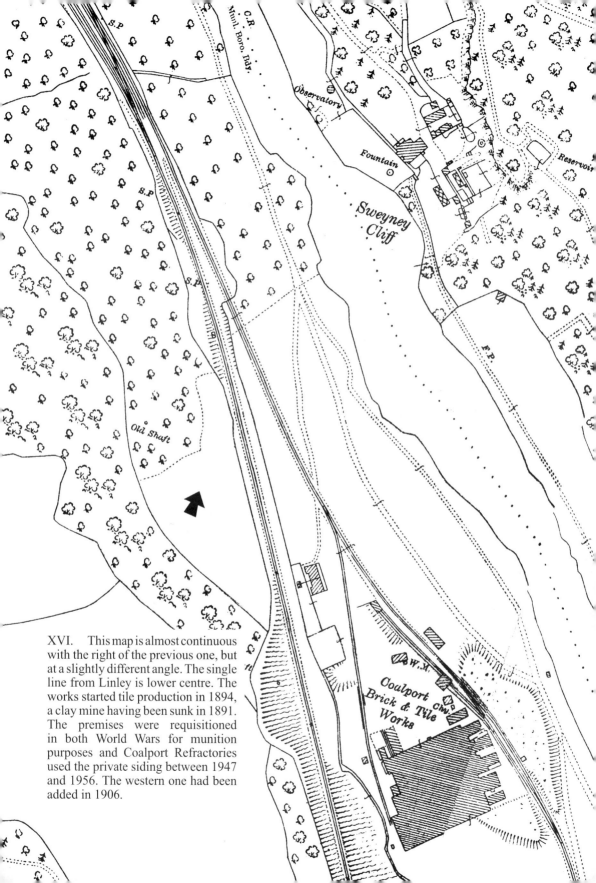

S.P.

C.R.
Mini. Boro. Bdy.

Observatory

Fountain

Reservoir

S.P.

Sweyney
Cliff

S.P.

F.P.

Old Shaft

XVI. This map is almost continuous
with the right of the previous one, but
at a slightly different angle. The single
line from Linley is lower centre. The
works started tile production in 1894,
a clay mine having been sunk in 1891.
The premises were requisitioned
in both World Wars for munition
purposes and Coalport Refractories
used the private siding between 1947
and 1956. The western one had been
added in 1906.

W.M.

Coalport
Brick & Tile
Works

86.   The loop and the platform on the left date from 1895. This was a peaceful location by the time that this photograph was taken in 1959. (Stations UK)

87.   In the distance is the 1895 signal box, which had 31 levers. The east end of the loop is out of sight. The platforms and buildings were not destroyed; the main one became a residence. (P.J.Garland/R.S.Carpenter coll.)

JACKFIELD HALT

88.   The first halt opened on 3rd December 1934, but the one seen was provided further south on 1st March 1954. The move was due to unstable ground. (Lens of Sutton coll.)

89.   Between the two halt sites was the works of Maw & Company producers of black glazed tiles. Their tramway crosses the bridge. There was a private siding for the works from 1877 to 1959; its ground frame is on the right, west of the line. Jackfield Sidings were further north, these serving tileries until 1958. (A.Dudman coll.)

IRONBRIDGE & BROSELEY

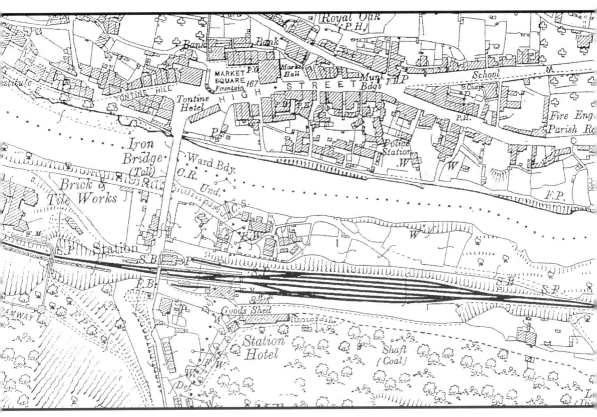

XVII. The 1902 survey reveals that the town was on the opposite side of the river, a handicap common on the SVR. Tolls on the bridge were another problem; they were not abolished until 1950. Ironbridge had a population of 3154 in 1861 and Broseley housed 4724.

90.   A westward view shows the position of the signal box from 1893; the previous one had been close by. There were 16 employees here in 1903, but around 20 in the 1930s.
(Lens of Sutton coll.)

91.   The box had 31 levers and was in use until 25th November 1956, when the down line and platform were taken out of use. This is from an Edwardian postcard in which the 2-4-0 is bound for Shrewsbury. (Lens of Sutton coll.)

92.   Abraham Darby pioneered the smelting of iron ore with coke made from coal, in 1709. His grandson (same name) cast the interlocking bridge components in the nearby Coalbrookdale Foundry. The bridge opened in 1781 and carried vehicles until 1931. It was photographed from the up platform in 1938 and is now a World Heritage Site. (D.K.Jones coll.)

Ironbridge & Broseley	1903	1913	1923	1933
Passenger tickets issued	29845	24247	32384	19195
Season tickets issued	*	*	108	55
Parcels forwarded	19240	19681	17827	21354
General goods forwarded (tons)	6751	6728	4866	3762
Coal and coke received (tons)	25881	23772	16182	13350
Other minerals received (tons)	4231	6334	4592	2698
General goods received (tons)	6369	7201	5580	3920
Trucks of livestock handled	85	60	24	13

(* not available)

93.   The photographer was slow with his shutter and did not date the picture. However, it includes the goods shed, the parcels shed and a view of the Ironbridge Gorge. The goods yard was open until 1st December 1963. (SLS coll.)

94.   No. 41203 runs in from Shrewsbury, sometime in 1962 and passes the base of the signal box. A ground frame had been placed outside its door. More of the gorge can be seen. The station site became a large car park. (A.W.V.Mace/Milepost 92½ coll.)

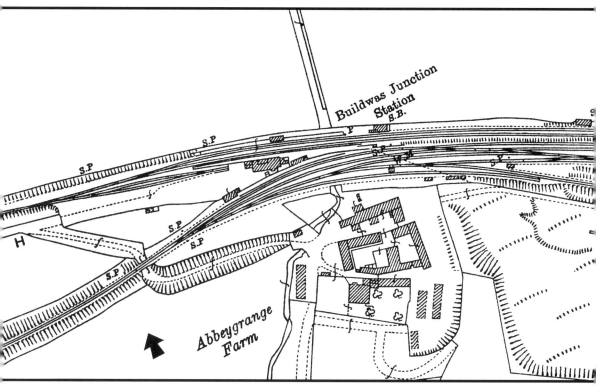

XVIII. The 1927 map has our route running from right to left. Lower left is the line to Much Wenlock and top right is a siding serving a pumping station. The upper two of the three tracks on the right are for Coalbrookdale trains. That route still serves Ironbridge Power Station, the branch starting at Madeley Junction, just east of Telford Central.

95.   A 1923 view westwards features the path between the Shrewsbury platform and the one for Wellington and Much Wenlock, left. Further left are the exchange sidings. (Stations UK)

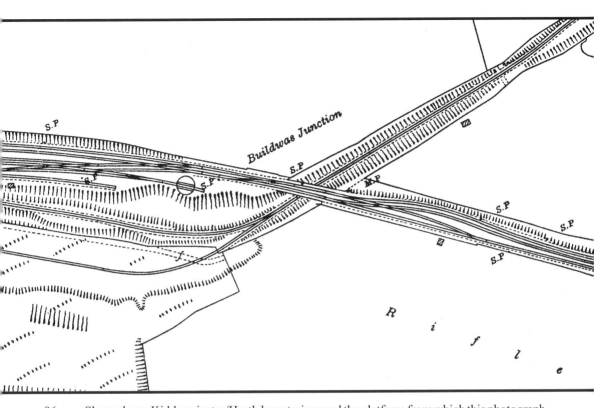

96.	Shrewsbury-Kidderminster/Hartlebury trains used the platform from which this photograph was taken in July 1954. Included is the third box, its final frame having an amazing 113 levers. This was in use from 9th December 1931 until 15th March 1964. (SLS coll.)

97.   Shunting signals are on the right as a railcar departs for Bridgnorth. The station area has become part of a golf course in recent years. The tracks north of the station were added in 1932. (A.J.B.Dodd/P.Chancellor coll.)

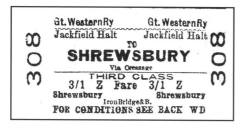

Gt. Western Ry   Gt. Western Ry
Jackfield Halt   Jackfield Halt
TO
SHREWSBURY
Via Cressage
THIRD CLASS
3/1   Z   Fare   3/1   Z
Shrewsbury   Shrewsbury
IronBridge&B.
FOR CONDITIONS SEE BACK   WD

308   308

Gt Western Ry   Gt Western Ry
Return Excursion   EXCURSION
HALF DAY   HALF DAY
RHYL to   Jackfield Halt to
JACKFIELD HALT   **RHYL**
Via Chester Wrexham   Via Cressage
& Cressage   Wrexham & Chester
THIRD CLASS   THIRD CLASS
IronBridge&B.   IronBridge&B.
FOR CONDITIONS   SEE BACK   W.D

082   082

98.   On the right is the dock and siding for local goods traffic, which ceased on 2nd December 1963. The train to Shrewsbury was hauled by 2-6-2T no. 4100 on 23rd April 1955. (H.F.Wheeller/R.S.Carpenter coll.)

99.   Viewed from the platform on the same day is one of the British Electricity Authority's Peckett 0-4-0STs shunting Ironbridge Power Station. The wagon tippler is on the right. Around 2500 tons of coal arrived daily, much of it from Highley. (H.F.Wheeller/R.S.Carpenter coll.)

100.   A snap from a train departing for Kidderminster on 22nd September 1958 has the Much Wenlock lines on the right. The furthest one was for goods traffic only. (H.C.Casserley)

101.   The first power station here opened in 1932 and the second in 1970. Much of it was built on former railway land. This is the scene on 24th April 1962. The road in the foreground ran to the village, which had 262 souls in 1901 and 329 in 1961. (B.W.L.Brooksbank)

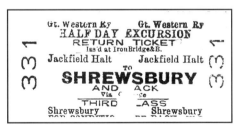

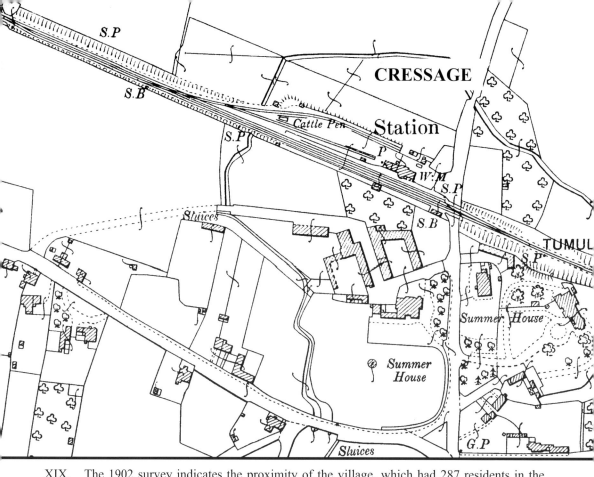

XIX.   The 1902 survey indicates the proximity of the village, which had 287 residents in the previous year. There were 350 in 1861 and 454 a century later.

102.   A loop, a second platform and a new signal box were provided in 1894. Here we see the east end of the station. There was a staff of three here in the 1920s and 30s. (SLS coll.)

103.   The main building is to the familiar design and the lamp hut was remote for safety reasons. The cats whiskers was a styling introduced by BR and also employed on the second generation of DMUs. (H.B.Priestley/Ted Hancock)

104.   The signal box was fitted with a gate wheel and a 23-lever frame. It closed on 2nd December 1963. The up waiting room was substantial for such a small population and is seen in 1961. (R.G.Nelson/T.Walsh coll.)

Cressage	1903	1913	1923	1933
Passenger tickets issued	13514	14353	12509	5830
Season tickets issued	*	*	49	22
Parcels forwarded	2692	4109	11119	3985
General goods forwarded (tons)	1195	1184	1087	156
Coal and coke received (tons)	793	748	284	69
Other minerals received (tons)	1673	1321	510	212
General goods received (tons)	1084	1546	1101	478
Trucks of livestock handled	38	134	56	67
(* not available)				

105.   No. 41304 was recorded with the 5.30pm from Shrewsbury on 28th August 1963. The two sidings had gone in the previous June. The main building survives as a dwelling. (D.Johnson)

COUND HALT

106.   The halt was situated at Coundlane, where the A458 takes to high ground. Cound Lodge Inn is on the left, as is the photographer's Hillman 10. The halt had opened on 4th August 1934, the year the car was made. (H.C.Casserley)

107.   The informal approach contains information for fishermen. In fact, most of the users of the halt were in this category, rather than local residents. (H.C.Casserley)

108.   The hotel also appears in picture 106 and this view shows the relationship and that this remote halt was electrically lit. The area became a beer garden. (R.M.Casserley)

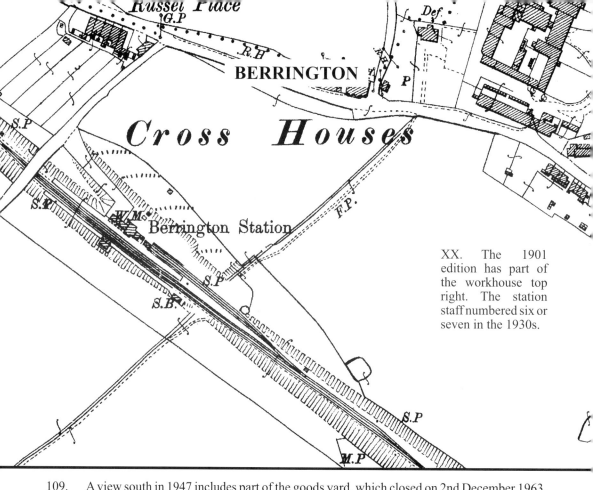

Russel Place
G.P

R.H

BERRINGTON

Def.

P

Cross Houses

S.P

S.P

S.P

W.M
Berrington Station

F.P.

S.P

S.B.

XX. The 1901 edition has part of the workhouse top right. The station staff numbered six or seven in the 1930s.

S.P

M.P

109.   A view south in 1947 includes part of the goods yard, which closed on 2nd December 1963. As elsewhere, a loop, extra platform and a new signal box arrived in 1894. One track remained open between Shrewsbury and Buildwas until 21st January 1968 for the conveyance of power station components too heavy for the bridge over the Severn on the branch from Madeley Junction. (Stations UK)

110. A train arrives from Shrewsbury, but no details survive. The station was extended to provide toilets, when the up platform was lengthened in 1894. The census recorded 928 in 1901, but this included the workhouse inmates numbering several hundred. (SLS coll.)

Berrington	1903	1913	1923	1933
Passenger tickets issued	16855	14073	9014	4811
Season tickets issued	*	*	14	19
Parcels forwarded	4695	6989	5380	2807
General goods forwarded (tons)	673	972	791	153
Coal and coke received (tons)	912	1727	1033	2369
Other minerals received (tons)	2441	1425	376	223
General goods received (tons)	1819	2090	1545	498
Trucks of livestock handled	209	175	31	8
(* not available)				

111. A stroll down the station approach allows us a glimpse of the weighbridge, the weigh house, the loading gauge and the lamp hut. The yard closed on 2nd February 1963 and the building later became a residence. (J.Moss/R.S.Carpenter coll.)

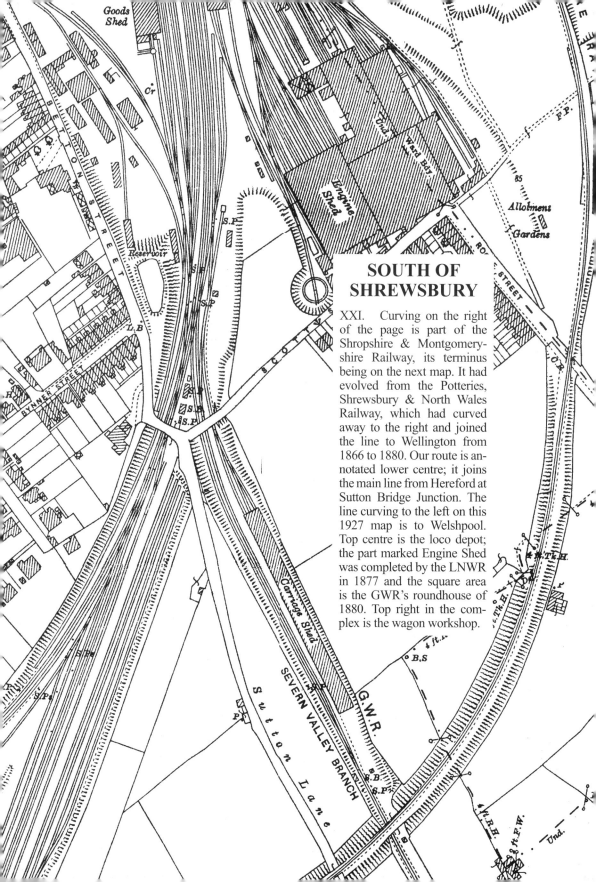

SOUTH OF SHREWSBURY

XXI.   Curving on the right of the page is part of the Shropshire & Montgomeryshire Railway, its terminus being on the next map. It had evolved from the Potteries, Shrewsbury & North Wales Railway, which had curved away to the right and joined the line to Wellington from 1866 to 1880. Our route is annotated lower centre; it joins the main line from Hereford at Sutton Bridge Junction. The line curving to the left on this 1927 map is to Welshpool. Top centre is the loco depot; the part marked Engine Shed was completed by the LNWR in 1877 and the square area is the GWR's roundhouse of 1880. Top right in the complex is the wagon workshop.

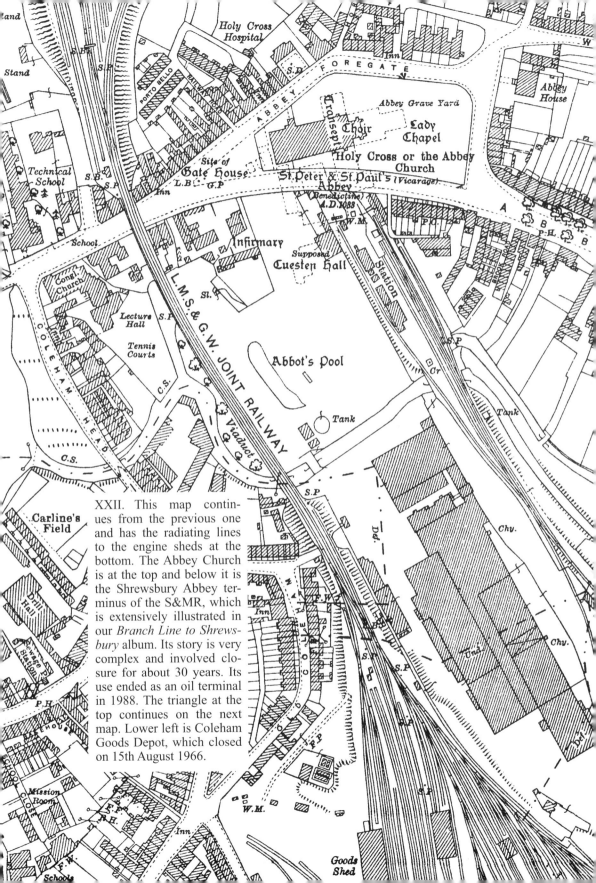

XXII. This map continues from the previous one and has the radiating lines to the engine sheds at the bottom. The Abbey Church is at the top and below it is the Shrewsbury Abbey terminus of the S&MR, which is extensively illustrated in our *Branch Line to Shrewsbury* album. Its story is very complex and involved closure for about 30 years. Its use ended as an oil terminal in 1988. The triangle at the top continues on the next map. Lower left is Coleham Goods Depot, which closed on 15th August 1966.

112.   This is Sutton Bridge Junction and the Severn Valley lines are lower left. Lower right is the carriage shed siding in this 1938 view. The 61-lever signal box was built in 1913 and was still in use in 2007. (D.K.Jones coll.)

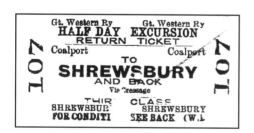

Gt. Western Ry   Gt. Western Ry
HALF DAY EXCURSION
RETURN   TICKET
Coalport   Coalport
TO
SHREWSBURY
AND BACK
Via Cressage
THIR   CLASS
SHREWSBUR   SHREWSBURY
FOR CONDITI   SEE BACK (W.L

Gt Western Ry.   Gt. Western Ry.
Cound Halt   Cound Halt
TO
BUILDWAS
THIRD   CLASS
8½d   Fare   8½d
Issued subject to the conditions & regulations set
out in the Companys Time Tables Bills & Notices
Buildwas   Buildwas
Cressage

113.   The shed code was 89A when photographed on 14th July 1963. It had been 84G from 1st January 1948, but became 6D from September 1963, when the LMR took over. There were 120 locos allocated here in 1950, but only 49 in 1965. The shedplate seen is 89D, which was Oswestry. (M.J.Stretton)

114.   The photograph is from 9th September 1966 and the end of steam here came on 5th March 1967. The diesel facilities on the left were not used after June 1970. This 70ft turntable replaced a 50ft one in LMS days, when the shed code was 4A. (J.H.Bamsey/D.H.Mitchell coll.)

SHREWSBURY

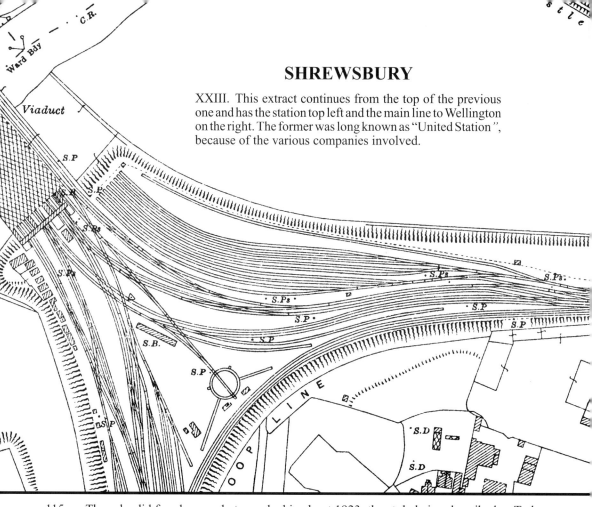

XXIII. This extract continues from the top of the previous one and has the station top left and the main line to Wellington on the right. The former was long known as "United Station", because of the various companies involved.

115. The splendid facade was photographed in about 1923, the style being described as Tudor Gothic. The approach road was lowered in 1901 to access a new subway and booking hall directly. Earlier there were direct crossings from the road to the platforms. The castle is on the right. (Stations UK)

116.   The LNWR built this massive signal box inside the triangle; it has a frame containing 180 levers and was still in use in 2007. The scene was recorded in 1959. The footbridge once linked platforms 2 to 9, but was removed. (Mowat coll./Brunel University)

117.   The roof over the southern part of the station was demolished in the Summer of 1963; much of the northern part had gone in 1931-32. The gas bottles are in place as 2-6-2T no. 41203 waits to leave for Kidderminster. (A.W.V.Mace/Milepost 92½)

118.   A train from Hereford rounds the curve towards platform 4. The signal box and Abbey Church are partially visible in this view from about 1964. The platforms had been renumbered in 1950. (Stations UK)

119.   The southern part of the station was built over the River Severn, the lattice structure being visible on the right of this 1966 panorama. The loco is hauling freight on the branch from Shropshire Union Yard, which closed on 5th April 1971. It is passing under Howard Street bridge, which was bricked up in 1985. (Stations UK)

120.   Main line diesel locomotives became common in the early 1960s and the LMR introduced Type 4s (class 47, as seen) around 1964. Its noise would not have impressed the rams on 16th September 1965. The caption could read "Brute force, brutes and a BRUTE".
(B.W.L.Brooksbank)

MP Middleton Press

EVOLVING THE ULTIMATE RAIL ENCYCLOPEDIA

Easebourne Lane, Midhurst, West Sussex.
GU29 9AZ Tel:01730 813169
www.middletonpress.co.uk email:info@middletonpress.co.uk
A-0 906520 B-1 873793 C-1 901706 D-1 904474

OOP Out of print at time of printing - Please check availability BROCHURE AVAILABLE SHOWING NEW TITLES